Original title:
Golden Horizon

Copyright © 2025 Creative Arts Management OÜ
All rights reserved.

Author: Levi Montgomery
ISBN HARDBACK: 978-1-80581-507-5
ISBN PAPERBACK: 978-1-80581-034-6
ISBN EBOOK: 978-1-80581-507-5

The Light that Guides

A beacon shines in the morning mist,
Frogs are croaking, they can't resist.
Chasing shadows all around,
Twirling hats, the best clowns found.

The sun's a friend with a gentle tease,
Bouncing rays with the greatest ease.
Socks are mismatched, it's quite absurd,
But laughter flows, no need for words.

A Journey Lit by Dawn's Glow

Woke up late, my toast is burned,
Coffee spills, oh how it churned!
Chasing light with a silly dash,
Trip on shoes, a comic crash!

Birds are laughing, I join in too,
Dancing shadows, just me and you.
With every step, there's giggles spread,
A joyful path, no fears to dread.

Beyond the Glimmering Edge

Past the hill where the sun will dive,
Silly hats where the squirrels thrive.
Jellybeans bounce from tree to tree,
   Nature's laugh is wild and free.

With every twirl, a chuckle gained,
Chasing dreams that are unchained.
Under the stars, we find our way,
Riding giggles till the break of day.

Dawn's Radiance

The rooster crows, a waking song,
As pajamas fly, all night feels wrong.
Coffee spills and pants worn low,
With sleepy grins, we steal the show.

A squirrel hops, a thief so spry,
Stealing snacks, oh my oh my!
The sun peeks in, a cheeky tease,
Bringing warmth with borrowed breeze.

Between Light and Sky

A bird drops by, with quite a flair,
And crapped upon my favorite chair.
With laughter shared, we clean the mess,
While giggles dance, we send our stress.

The clouds today wear silly hats,
And rainbows whisper to the cats.
Between bright hues, we chase the fun,
In colors bold, we laugh and run.

The Sun's Embrace

The beach ball flies, we jump and dive,
While sunscreen hugs us, we survive.
Sandy snacks find footing wrong,
And seagulls join our silly song.

With laughter loud, the waves applaud,
As cousins bicker, we call it odd.
Warmth drapes us like a cozy wrap,
In sunlit rays, we take a nap.

A Tapestry of Dusk

The sky erupts in shades of fry,
While fireflies twinkle, oh me, oh my!
Picnic crumbs attract the ants,
As laughter rolls and humor dances.

With nighttime smells, we gather round,
To tell bad jokes, our silly sound.
Stars appear, a winking game,
In twilight's glow, it's never the same.

Veils of Radiance at Dusk

As day retreats, the sun throws a fit,
Bouncing like a child, won't you admit?
The clouds wear shades, a fashion delight,
Dancing in colors, the sky's party night.

With llamas in hats sipping golden tea,
And squirrels tap-dancing on branches with glee,
The moon pulls a prank, winks down at us,
While stars play hide-and-seek, oh, what a fuss!

Radiance at Dawn

A rooster croaks tunes, the sun's sleepy rise,
It yawns so loud, you'd think it's no surprise.
Pancakes flip-flop, syrup takes a dive,
In the breakfast club, everyone's alive!

Coffee spills laughter, mugs clink with cheer,
While toast pops up like it's had too much beer,
Morning's a circus, bright and absurd,
As nature giggles, the day's word is heard!

The Luminous Edge

On the cliff's edge, a squirrel takes flight,
With dreams of acorns, oh what a sight!
He trips on a twig, does a somersault spin,
Lands in a bush—where the laughter begins!

The sun winks at birds, soaring up high,
Giving them sunglasses, they laugh in the sky,
Clouds are the pillows, soft and so sweet,
As they drift on by, it's a fluffy retreat!

Glistening Dreams Await

In the puddles' mirror, reflections so bold,
Fish sing like rockstars, their scales gleam like gold.
A cat wearing boots joins the watery band,
Flipping his tail, he takes a brave stand.

Rainbows on scooters zip past in a rush,
While bananas in pajamas cause quite the fuss,
Under the sparkle of dew on a leaf,
The world spins in laughter, oh what a relief!

Awakening Skies

The sun rolled out of bed, yelling loud,
With pajamas made of clouds, feeling proud.
Coffee spills on the morning dew,
"Oops! Sorry, nature! Didn't mean to brew!"

Birds threw a party, with hats all askew,
Chirping jokes only they seem to construe.
A squirrel danced, tail sharp as a knife,
While flowers laughed, saying, "This is our life!"

The Breath of Daylight

Morning stretched on a comfy old chair,
Brushing off dreams with a tousle of hair.
A pancake flipped, creating a scene,
"Not my fault! I'm just trying to be lean!"

The jam jar jived, it was ready to break,
Telling the toast, "I'm your favorite mistake!"
Sunbeams tickled the sleepy-eyed cat,
As she swatted shadows, exclaiming, "What's that!?"

Illuminating the Unknown

A shadow creeps like a clumsy old fool,
Tripping on the light, feeling like a tool.
"Who turned the lights on?" it grumbled aloud,
While the lantern chuckled, feeling quite proud.

Ghosts in the corner were playing charades,
Throwing silly faces, not caring who fades.
One whispered, "Boo!" but forgot the rest,
Leaving everyone laughing, enjoying their jest!

Dreams Touched by Light

A dream with a mustache danced on a star,
Sipping on moonbeams from a candy jar.
"Why's the sky purple?" it asked with a grin,
"Because the sun's tickling! Now let's begin!"

With jellybean quips and a sprinkle of cheer,
The night giggled softly, no worries or fear.
So let's chase the giggles, let dreams take flight,
In a world of wonder, where jokes shine bright!

Glimmering Futures

A squirrel wore shades, so slick,
He planned to sell acorns quick.
Under the sun, he struck a pose,
While the chickens rolled their toes.

A cat in flip-flops strolled by,
Yelling, "Why not touch the sky?"
He tripped on a leaf, oh dear,
Laughed as he fell, "Next year, my fear!"

The Horizon's Dance

Two penguins boogied on ice,
Claiming they'd win the dance prize.
Out popped a seal with a grin,
Said, "Let's dance, where do I begin?"

They spun and twirled, what a sight!
Falling over in sheer delight.
A walrus joined, with a flair,
'Twas a wiggly frolic affair!

Awakening the Cosmos

Aliens landed, oh what fun,
Offering donuts, by the ton.
They giggled and danced, all around,
Spinning in circles, then fell down.

One asked for coffee, strong and hot,
Earthlings replied with, "You've got
To try our chocolate with sprinkles!"
Alien grinned, saying, "I love crinkles!"

Celestial Pathways

Stars played hopscotch in the night,
Creating a game that felt just right.
Planets wore hats, and floated by,
Shouting, "Come join! Don't be shy!"

A comet zoomed with a tail so bright,
Flipping pancakes, what a sight!
Space was filled with laughter and cheer,
As astronauts danced without fear.

Skies Painted with Promise

Bright hues splash across the sky,
Chickens in pajamas wonder why.
A cow dreams of gold, quite a sight,
While clouds giggle, taking flight.

Sunbeams tickle trees with cheer,
Squirrels plot mischief, never fear.
A rabbit hops in polka dots,
While shadows dance with silly thoughts.

Celestial Reverie

Stars in skirts parade around,
The moon trips over moonlit ground.
Comets with roller skates zoom,
Spreading laughter within the gloom.

Galaxies play peek-a-boo,
As planets wear hats, just for you.
An astronaut swaps drinks with a cat,
Creating chaos where they're at.

When Light Enfolds the World

The sun bursts forth, a custard pie,
Dropping crumbs from way up high.
Rabbits with shades sip lemonade,
While daydreams in happy shades parade.

The breeze hums tunes of old-timey jazz,
Birds breakdance, creating a pizzazz.
In the field, a loaf of bread acts grand,
As ants hold a feast, a wondrous band.

Brushstrokes of Dawn

Morning paints the town with glee,
Cats on skateboards chase a bee.
Pigs in capes fly through the air,
While coffee cups sing without a care.

The rooster's voice is a wobbly tune,
As it moonwalks under the buffoon moon.
Today's menu? A slice of fun,
As laughter sparkles like the sun.

The Dawn Unfolds

When morning breaks with quite a grin,
The sun leaps up, let the fun begin!
I spill my coffee, it splashes bright,
But who needs pants in this soft sunlight?

The rooster crows, "Time to awake!"
I toss a sock; it lands on the lake.
Chasing the cat seems like a sport,
But she just naps, the lazy sort!

Pathways of Illumination

On pathways paved with buttered toast,
I skip and trip, a clumsy host.
The path ahead is lined with cheese,
I smile and munch, "Oh, if you please!"

A squirrel jogs by, decked in a hat,
He nods at me; what's up with that?
Chasing shadows, we race in glee,
He wins the dash—oh, let me be!

Luminous Futures

In futures bright, where jokes abound,
I tell a pun, and laughter's found.
The sun is plush, like cotton candy,
When clouds float by, all big and dandy.

We ride on beams, like silly fools,
In pajamas, while we break the rules.
With light as our guide, we dance and sing,
Together we make the whole world bling!

A World Bathed in Light

In a world where brightness makes us giddy,
We wear our shades—oh, isn't life witty?
The shadows play tricks, they dance and prance,
I trip on a cloud, my goofy chance!

The balloons float high, creating a scene,
With giggles and grins, we look so keen.
Our carefree antics shine like the day,
As we bounce around in a sunlit play!

The Light that Beckons

In the morning sun, I lost my hat,
Chasing shadows like a playful cat.
The birds all laughed, gave me a wink,
With every step, I felt the clink!

A dog decided to join my quest,
Rolling in puddles, oh what a jest!
The sunbeam giggled with all its might,
As I tripped over my shoelace in flight.

A squirrel darted, we had a race,
I almost thought I'd keep up the pace.
But with a whoosh, it raced up a tree,
Left me laughing, oh woe is me!

In the cheerful glow, I twirled around,
Creating a dance, where joy is found.
Each chuckle echoed as I pranced,
In light's embrace, I took my chance!

Wings of Brilliant Light

Oh, how the daylight brings a grin,
Butterflies flapping, they know I'm in.
With every flutter, my heart does sway,
The garden's party starts the day!

The bees are buzzing, hitting the beat,
Trying to dance on my two left feet.
I stepped on a flower, oh what a sight,
The petals giggled in sheer delight!

A rainbow formed out of coffee foam,
Who knew that breakfast could feel like home?
I raised my cup to the vibrant sky,
And spilled my drink—oh my, oh my!

So here I am in a joyful spin,
With laughter echoing within my skin.
The world's a canvas, so bright and true,
In wings of light, I'll fly with you!

Journey Towards the Morning

Off to the dawn, I've packed my dreams,
With socks that clash, or so it seems.
A llama waved as I strolled by,
Winking, it seemed to be quite spry!

The road had puddles that dared my shoes,
With every splash, I just couldn't lose.
Giggles danced in the drops of dew,
And sunflower faces were cheering too!

A cat on a fence gave me a stare,
As if to say, 'Life's not that rare!'
I offered a wave, it blinked with flair,
Proclaiming, 'In fun, we both must share!'

With each small step, I felt elated,
The morning light, it felt fated.
And as I walked towards the day's embrace,
I wore my joy like a shining face!

Threads of Sunlit Moments

In pockets of sun, I found some socks,
One blue, one red, oh what a paradox!
I wore them proudly, oh what a sight,
The fashion police would take flight!

Chasing a bubble that danced in the breeze,
I leapt like a frog, with utmost ease.
With every pop, I laughed out loud,
Who knew joy could attract a crowd?

Sipping lemonade under a tree,
I spilled some juice—oh do not see!
The ants had a feast, they cheered and danced,
They knew well that summer chanced!

So here's to the threads of these bright days,
With laughter interwoven in countless ways.
Let whimsy lead in the light's embrace,
For every moment holds a trace!

The Edge of Daydreams

In the land where wishes fly,
Chickens wear hats, don't ask me why.
Birds sing tunes in clumsy dance,
While squirrels plot their next romance.

Clouds giggle as they change their shape,
A pancake sun, a syrup drape.
Rainbows prance like silly fools,
While ducks read books in sparkling pools.

Daydreams flutter like butterflies,
Whispering jokes, oh such surprise!
A tree recites a funny rhyme,
As shadows work overtime.

Laughter twirls on a breeze so light,
Tickling noses, oh what a sight!
Beneath this canvas of delight,
We chase the sun with all our might.

Sunlit Reflections

Mirrors dance in the summer glow,
Fish wear ties, and cows play fo' show.
The sun gives winks, oh what a tease,
While ants hold hands with utmost ease.

Bubbles float with a giggle and sway,
Skating through the sky, come what may.
A cat on a surfboard rides the breeze,
While bees play chess among the trees.

Shadows moonwalk on grass so green,
Silly bugs join in, what a scene!
The flowers shout, "We're feeling fine!"
As butterflies sip on fruit punch wine.

A pool of giggles sprawls on the ground,
Every corner filled with joyful sound.
In reflections of a sunny spree,
We laugh at all that we can see.

Chasing the Last Glimmer

A sloth in shades lounges on a leaf,
While turtles plan a heist for a brief.
The sun waves bye, with a cheeky grin,
And fireflies goof up, with a spin.

Kites fly high, pulling strings of fate,
While dogs wear goggles, thinking it's fate.
The horizon blushes, a dazzling show,
As frogs in tuxedos steal the glow.

Chasing flickers, we trip on air,
Jumping over shadows without a care.
Laughter bubbles, like soda pop,
As we dance on clouds, right to the top.

With a last sigh, the day takes a bow,
Balloons go wild, cows start to meow.
In this playful chase, so light,
We stumble home 'neath the twinkling night.

Beneath a Canvas of Light

Under a sky where giggles reside,
A unicorn rides a bicycle wide.
Crayons draw the clouds in a swirl,
While mermaids practice the latest twirl.

Clocks melt down like ice cream drips,
As monkeys on roller skates do flips.
The evening hums a funny tune,
While the stars compete with a smiling moon.

Colors splash in a joyful race,
Pigs in top hats take first place.
The canvas stretches, full of dreams,
As laughter flows in wild streams.

Beneath this vault of glowing cheer,
A trampoline of hugs appears near.
We leap and bounce, all worries out,
Wrapped in the joy, we laugh and shout.

When Light Breaks Free

The sun pops up like toast,
A gleeful little host.
It spills its jam worldwide,
While I dance, arms open wide.

Waking dreams, oh what a sight,
Bedhead hair, a funny fright.
With coffee brewing in the pot,
The morning laughs, it hits the spot.

The streetlights blink their last goodbyes,
As silly clouds race through the skies.
Birds chirp tunes that tickle my ear,
I giggle, as the day draws near.

In this glow, mischief's set free,
No one knows how bright we'll be.
We'll bounce around, play and shout,
As light spills in, there's no doubt.

A Tapestry of Dawn

Threads of sunlight weave and twist,
In this fabric, joy can't be missed.
The colors dance and jiggle about,
With laughter loud, we jump and shout.

Flowers yawn, stretch in the light,
Waking up with pure delight.
Bees buzz around like tiny drones,
Playing tag, stealing tones of groans.

Socks mismatched, I'm dressed in flair,
Chasing shadows without a care.
The sun flips pancakes on the sky,
While every cloud just woefully sighs.

With every ray, the silliness blooms,
A parade of joy fills all the rooms.
In this quilt where laughter is spun,
What a riot, oh what fun!

Horizon of Endless Light

A gleam that's silly, bright, and bold,
A sunrise joke that never grows old.
Chasing shadows, it trip, it slips,
As giggles spill from beatific lips.

The world wakes up in a playful whirl,
Each moment, a wild, whimsical twirl.
Socks on the wrong feet, birds dressed in hats,
The sun chuckles, warming up the spats.

As laughter bubbles rise and pop,
A giant coffee cup won't stop.
Days like these are endless delight,
With an endless glow, our futures are bright.

Every sunrise, a slip and a slide,
With jests in the air, there's nowhere to hide.
If life gives you light, just don't take it slow,
Join in the frolics, let the good times flow!

The Warmth of Breaking Day

Rooster crows with a silly grin,
The day begins, let the fun begin!
Toast and jam can't wait to play,
While I giggle at the sunny display.

Pajamas still on, messy hair fluffed,
Trips to the fridge are so delightfully stuffed.
The sun shines in, a playful tease,
Reminding us all to do as we please.

Cars honk like clowns on parade,
The city wakes up, don't be afraid.
With every smile that passes my way,
The warmth of life insists on staying today.

So bring on the blunders, the joyful spree,
When light unfurls, it's wild and free.
With a wink and a nudge, we close the night,
And snuggle the stars, oh what a sight!

Sunlit Promises

Beneath the beams, the shadows dance,
Squirrels in hats, they take a chance.
A sunbeam's wink, a giggle in flight,
Even the grass is wearing delight.

Jellybeans tumble from cherry trees,
Ticklish breezes provoke some wheezes.
While daisies plot a mischievous coup,
Petals giggle, 'Let's paint the dew!'

The clouds wear tie-dye, silly and bright,
Gathering stories of sheer delight.
A sunbeam's warmth, with a wink and a jest,
Inviting all to join this jest.

So grab your shades and wear a grin,
Let laughter sway, let the fun begin!
In fields of joy, where the heart turns bold,
We weave our tales in the sun's warm gold.

Threads of Amber Sky

Up in the air, a kite takes flight,
Chasing clouds in a ridiculous fight.
With tails of laughter, it's hard to trace,
How many giggles can fill one space?

The sun in a bowtie, quite dapper and fine,
Winks at the moon, 'I'll meet you at nine.'
While clouds play poker, in laughter they sigh,
As we sit below, with apple pie.

Hedges were sneezing, with blooms in a fit,
With bees telling jokes, they just can't sit.
Their buzzing chorus, a symphony loud,
Tickles the senses of every proud cloud.

So dance in the sunlight, don't take it too deep,
For life's little moments, we joyfully keep.
Every ray, a thread in this ludicrous sky,
We find laughter's fabric as days pass us by.

Journeys Beneath the Ember

There's a road of giggles where we now tread,
With socks on our hands, and hats on our head.
We dodge the puddles, that splash like a tease,
And dance with the daisies, if you please.

The sun paints the pavement with laughter and glee,
While the trees play charades, look over and see!
With hidden umbrellas, they sway and they joke,
As if to say, 'Why not dance with a bloke?'

A squirrel in a scarf, he's leading the way,
To the land of 'Why not!' where jokes never stray.
With hiccups of laughter, an unexpected show,
This journey's the best, with much more to grow.

So come down the path, with a skip and a whirl,
Let's twirl with the butterflies, give laughter a twirl.
Where every step holds a humorous spark,
Together we chuckle till the day turns dark.

Awakening in Sun's Embrace

The morning giggles from an early ray,
As sunshine tickles, it leads the way.
With sleepy yawns, the flowers rise,
Searching for mischief beneath the skies.

A rooster in sunglasses, what a sight,
Crowls out a tune, with pure delight.
While pancakes flip over, the syrup flows,
It's breakfast time, let the giggle train go!

Worms in a conga line, wiggling along,
They've decided a party is never wrong.
The grasshoppers hum their peculiar tune,
While the sun beams down, laughing at noon.

Celebrate life in this silly embrace,
With sunshine and laughter, life's a grand chase.
So roll in the grass, let joy take the lead,
In the warmth of the sun, we are all freed!

The Spectrum of Dawn

A rooster crows, his voice a song,
As kitchen pans declare what's wrong.
With slippers on and hair askew,
I wonder if today's a zoo.

The toast pops up, a dance of bread,
While cat plots mischief in my bed.
The sun peeks through with a sly grin,
Looks like the party's about to begin.

Coffee brews, a steamy show,
With caffeine high, I'm ready to go!
But where did I put my other shoe?
The day's gone wild, who knew this view?

In pajamas still, I step outside,
The neighbor's dog is my new guide.
With each step, I trip and tumble,
At least today, there's room to stumble.

Morning's Radiant Whisper

A squirrel dances on the fence,
Mocking my morning pretense.
With sunlight warming up the street,
I wonder if I've eaten meat?

My coffee's gone, my pants are too,
But hey, I've got a sky of blue.
The birds are chirping, what a sight,
I wave to them, it feels so right.

In yoga pants, I greet the day,
While my dog snickers, "Let's play!"
With every step, I prance and leap,
But tripping twice, I lose my sleep.

With giggles echoing wide and far,
I find my joy in this bizarre.
The morning's charm, a playful tease,
Who knew fun could come with ease?

Shining Moments Ahead

In the bright light, I stumble forth,
Awake and lost, I seek my worth.
The pancakes flip like acrobats,
Unsure if I'm on track with that.

The dog has claimed my cozy chair,
As I negotiate with a glare.
"Just one more slice," the cake does call,
I swear I had it all in the hall.

My neighbor waves, a morning sight,
Sporting socks of neon light.
We chat about our dreams and schemes,
While I try to sip through buttered dreams.

The sun climbs high, it brings a cheer,
As I embrace the day, my dear.
With laughter loud and spirits bright,
These shining moments feel just right!

Echoes of Twilight's Kiss

The day winds down, but who's to say,
The night won't dance in a funny way?
With shadows long and laughter near,
I chase the dusk, fueled by cheer.

A firefly flits, a little sprite,
Winking as it takes off on flight.
I try to catch it, full of grace,
But end up tangled, oh what a face!

The stars are out, they burst and glow,
But isn't that cupcake worth a throw?
With crumbs in hand, I twirl around,
In this odd party, joy is found.

Through quirky night, I dance and play,
With echoes ringing, all the way.
The twilight's kiss, a silly tease,
I end the night with giggles and breeze.

Echoes of the Setting Sun

The sun slips down, like a clumsy cat,
Chasing shadows, oh where is it at?
Bouncing birds laugh, in their feathered shoes,
While squirrels join in, with their zany moves.

The sky blushes red, like a joke gone wrong,
As clouds gather round, singing a silly song.
A rabbit hops close, with a wink and a grin,
Saying, 'Did you hear? The sun's had too much gin!'

Waves wiggle and giggle, on a sandy beach,
As starfish applaud, without even a speech.
The day waves goodbye, in a silly parade,
And the moon rolls in, feeling slightly betrayed.

With a chuckle the stars twinkle bright,
As night winks at day, what a curious sight!
They dance in a circle, a nightly refrain,
And all of our laughter spills out like champagne.

The Glow of New Beginnings

A new dawn breaks, with a wink and a tease,
As roosters crow loud, 'Get up! If you please!'
The sun yawns and stretches, with a goofy gleam,
While coffee cups giggle, in a morning dream.

Butterflies flit, in their sparkly coats,
While frogs quack out loud, in their finest goats.
A squirrel shouts, 'Hey, is this show time?'
And the flowers all bloom, in perfect rhyme.

As raindrops tap dance, on windowpanes bright,
The world spins 'round with a comical light.
The clouds play hide and seek, oh what a sight,
While the sun plays the part, of a playful knight!

With each giggle, the day takes its flight,
Embracing the silly, the warm, and the bright.
We wink at the sky, with a smile on our face,
For every new morning is a joyful embrace.

Beyond the Distant Glow

Far off where the colors begin to collide,
Raccoons in tuxedos put on quite the ride.
They sip on sweet nectar, with hats on their heads,
While silly old cows joke about their own sheds.

The fireflies flash, like a disco gone wild,
Chasing their tails, just like a lost child.
In the distance, a bear tries to juggle some fruit,
While owls hoot softly, in their best suited loot.

The sun takes a bow, as it winks at the morn,
And all the critters shout, 'Oh look, it's reborn!'
With laughter a-plenty, they twirl in the day,
In a world so whimsical, they all love to play.

Beyond the bright glow, there's a cake made of cheer,
With sprinkles of joy, and silly old beer.
As daylight unfurls, laughter fills up the air,
With each little moment, oh how we all share!

Where Daybreak Meets the Sea

At dawn the waves giggle, like a child at play,
As seagulls crack jokes, flying high on display.
The sands tell tall tales, in whispers and sighs,
While crabs dance a jig, beneath blue-sky highs.

A lighthouse spins round, like an old disco ball,
Waving its arms, saying, 'Hey! Look at all!'
The sun winks at fishermen, casting their nets,
As dolphins jump in, with the best little pets.

The surfboards all race, in a friendly debate,
While pirates pretend, they're just out for a plate.
A tide pool declares, 'I'm the best in the show!'
As the ocean giggles, with a bubbly glow.

With seashells for hats, and seaweed for ties,
They celebrate dawn, under colorful skies.
In the mix of laughter, where night turns to play,
Daybreak meets the sea, in a whimsically way.

Flowers of Morning's Light

In the garden of giggles, they bloom,
Petals like smiles, chasing away gloom.
Bees wear tiny hats, buzzing in style,
While daisies dance and tickle a smile.

Sunshine spills laughter, on dewdrops bright,
Worms throw a party, in soil delight.
Butterflies flutter, with jokes they share,
Even the lettuce is caught in a stare.

Morning stretches, yawning wide in cheer,
Birds sing punchlines only you can hear.
Clouds wear sunglasses, sipping on tea,
As flowers chuckle, 'Is it just me?'

So here's to the blooms, with humor so light,
Every petal a giggle, every stem a sight.
In this garden of joy, let's dance and sway,
For laughter is blooming, come join the play!

The Edge of Infinity

At the brink of the world, we tiptoe near,
Counting our toes, with a sprinkle of cheer.
Why is the sky so big and so blue?
An angel in flip-flops, is this really true?

Stars up above, they've had too much fun,
Swapping their places, a cosmic run.
The moon's in pajamas, dreaming of cheese,
While comets do cartwheels, dashing with ease.

Time plays practical jokes from afar,
Tick-tock and giggle, like a goofy car.
In the land of unknown, we float like a kite,
With laughter that echoes into the night.

So let's leap from the edge, toss worries away,
Around us the magic, like children at play.
In the dance of the cosmos, we'll spin and twine,
On the edge of forever, where silliness shines!

Light's Embrace

A beam through the window, tickles my nose,
Light dances in sparkles, as the curtains do pose.
It stretches and yawns, with a hint of a grin,
Whispering secrets, how long has it been?

Shadows are giggling, in corners they hide,
Waiting for sunlight, to sweep them outside.
Together they chase, with a hop and a bounce,
While lights cast tall tales, as laughter pounces.

The chandelier winks, with a spark of delight,
"We're all just here for the fun, am I right?"
A sunbeam trips over, landing on a cat,
Who purrs and rolls over, "Now, how 'bout that!"

So raise up your glasses, to the glow all around,
In this bright little chaos, true joy can be found.
Here's to the warmth, the laughter's embrace,
Where silliness flowers, in every warm space!

Daybreak's Gentle Call

A rooster in slippers, begins with a song,
"Wake up, sleepyheads, you've snoozed far too long!"
He struts down the lane, like a champion proud,
While the sun lifts its head, through a fluffy cloud.

Coffee beans giggle, as they splash in a cup,
While toast starts to dance, saying, "Eat me up!"
Muffins wave warmly, like newly made friends,
In this breakfast delight, the laughter never ends.

Outside butterflies, on a trampoline play,
While flowers are inline-skating, hip-hip hooray!
Every chirp from a sparrow, bursts with a joke,
As the day breaks forth, in a soft, happy cloak.

So let's grab our hats, and dance through the morn,
In this whimsical world, where laughter is born.
Each dawn brings a smile, with its gentle call,
In the silly embrace, there's enough joy for all!

The Lure of Distant Light

A flicker twinkled in the air,
A glowing orb beyond compare.
I tripped on clouds, fell with delight,
Chasing sparkles, oh what a sight!

The sun had plans, but I was late,
With sandwiches and plans for fate.
I called my friends, they brought their laughs,
We ate warm toast, and planned our gaffs!

When shadows danced, we joined the game,
"Why are we here?" became our claim.
So here we sit, with laughter bright,
At sunset's lure, we seem so light!

A Pathway of Sunbeams

Follow the trail of buttered beams,
Where sunlight bounces like funny dreams.
We skipped and hopped, our shadows ran,
In a line formed like a marching band!

Each step a giggle, a light-hearted roar,
Until we bumped into a flapping door.
A chicken crossed, it squawked and quacked,
'There's no way you'll catch me, I'm well packed!'

With fluffy tails, we chased it fast,
Circling back, what a comical blast!
With sunbeams as guides, we danced around,
On this wacky road, joy abounds!

Radiant Whispers in Twilight

As dusk approached and giggles soared,
Whispers of light, we all adored.
A sneaky breeze played tricks on us,
With every step, we burst in fuss!

Twilight painted with colors bright,
We tried to dance, but tripped in fright.
With laughter bubbling, we fell in heaps,
In this odd world, joy leaps and creeps!

The moon appeared, with a wink so sly,
"Catch me if you can!" it seemed to cry.
With shadows in tow, we played with glee,
In the fading glow, how funny we be!

The Painted Skies

Oh look, the sky's a giant pasty,
With swirls and twirls, it looks so hasty.
We set our brushes to stroke the hue,
But spilled the paint, oh what a view!

The clouds turned polka dot and stripe,
Creating patterns, not what we liked.
With each splatter, we laughed anew,
Our masterpiece seemed to think it flew!

As colors blended, we sat and grinned,
A canvas born of silenced wind.
With a wink to the moon, we took a bow,
For in our art, we felt the wow!

Where Light Meets the Sky

The sun wears shades, what a sight,
It caught a cloud in a friendly fight.
Birds donned tuxedos, ready to sing,
Chasing the rays like a springy thing.

A squirrel danced on the power line,
Thinking it's a crusty grapevine.
Pitching a fit with a goofy cheer,
Forgetting the world, filling the sphere.

The sun slipped on banana peels,
Wobbling with laughter, how it squeals!
With every bounce, the grass goes "whoa!"
Pulling pranks while the breezes blow.

And who knew clouds could be so sly?
Making shapes of a pizza pie.
With a wink and a twirl, it's all okay,
Under this laughter-filled sunlit display.

Sunlit Whispers

A beaming grin stretched far and wide,
As the sun decided to take a ride.
With pancakes flipping from its rays,
It served up laughter on sunny days.

Chirping crickets wore tiny hats,
Holding court with a parade of cats.
They danced in circles, oh what a scene!
Riding on sunbeams, all dressed in green.

A rabbit juggled with shiny pebbles,
While the wind told jokes with merry levels.
The world erupted in gleeful cheer,
As sunlight painted all that was near.

Bright colors splashed on every wall,
As the cheeky shadows began to sprawl.
The day bowed down with a chuckle and sigh,
Wrapping the world in a roguish sky.

A Brush of Dawn's Light

The rooster's horn blew a raspy tune,
While dawn tiptoed in with a silver spoon.
It painted the world with pancake hue,
And tickled the grass, how it gleamed anew.

A hedgehog slipped on a slice of bread,
With jam and butter on its head.
Rolling down the hill with a giggle,
While daisies swayed, the sun's warm wiggle.

Butterflies in corsets, such a sight!
Twisted like ballerinas taking flight.
They flounced and fluttered, quite the show,
Whispering secrets that only they know.

And as the day drank its morning tea,
The clouds made faces, carefree and free.
Each moment tickled the edge of delight,
In the chuckling glow of the soft twilight.

The Glorious Awakening

A rooster crowed as if on cue,
Waking up the crew in blue.
The sun waltzed in with its sunny flair,
Rolling back curtains, lifting the air.

A dog did a jig, its tail in a spin,
While the cat looked on, bearing a grin.
Together they laughed at what life could be,
In a symphony of sun with a sprinkle of glee.

Dewdrops chuckled on the tulip's head,
Whispering stories of the night that fled.
The sun tickled each leaf, and oh what fun,
Painting the earth with a palette of sun.

So here's to the day, with all of its quirks,
The tickling rays that dance and lurk.
In every corner, there's laughter and play,
As the sky bursts forth with a goofy display.

Light against the Shadows

A flicker of light breaks the gloom,
Dancing around like a disco ball's boom.
Shadows retreat with a comical fright,
Arm-in-arm, they take their flight.

Sunbeams giggle, they tickle the trees,
While shadows squirm, like they're stung by bees.
The world laughs loud, as the night takes a seat,
What silliness lurks in this sunlight's beat!

It's a showdown of heights, in the bright of the day,
The dark makes a face, then melts away.
With every cackle, the light draws near,
Who knew sunlight could hold such cheer?

So here's to the rays that chase away dread,
While shadows hide, and the light forms a bed.
We'll toast to the laughter and joy that they bring,
In a world where both shadow and sun dance and sing.

The Rise of a New Day

The rooster crows like a rock star on scene,
Morning spills forth, bright and keen.
Coffee brews with a aromatic thrill,
While sleepy heads are a bit less still.

Pajamas are worn like crowns of delight,
As daybreak arrives, what a marvelous sight!
Eggs start to sizzle, they pop and they roll,
Kitchen chaos takes its humorous toll.

Cats leap about with the grace of a king,
While dogs chase their tails, what a funny fling!
Sunshine peeks in, through the curtains it prances,
With all this commotion, who still takes their chances?

So let's raise a toast to this whimsical morn,
When laughter and mischief are freshly reborn.
With snacks on the table and cheer in the air,
New day, new tales, nothing can compare!

Celestial Glow

Stars wink at me from their cushioned space,
Giggling softly, in an interstellar race.
The moon wears a hat that's too large for its head,
And calls out for laughter instead of dread.

Comets dart by like a flash of light,
Shooting through the cosmos, quite a sight!
They leave trails of giggles and fairy-tale dust,
In this vast universe, it's laughter we trust.

Planets chat gossip in whispers of ray,
While asteroids tumble, in a tumble of play.
What a ridiculous scene in the twilight so bright,
As astrophysics takes flight with the moon's secret sprite!

So look up tonight and find joy in the stars,
Let laughter abound from Venus to Mars.
In this celestial glow, we all share a laugh,
For who knew the cosmos could craft such a path?

A Promise of Dawn

Morning whispers secrets in soft, bright hues,
As sheep count people, how silly it muse.
The sun takes a stretch, yawns wide with a grin,
While dew-dropped flowers begin their daydream spin.

Birds burst with laughter, their songs weave delight,
While rabbits giggle, bounding left and right.
Balloons filled with giggles float high up above,
As nature cracks jokes, sharing warmth and love.

Sunshine rolls in on a donut-shaped beam,
Uncle Fog tiptoes, avoiding an ice cream dream.
With trees wearing hats made of foliage bright,
It's a circus of joy that bursts into sight!

So here's to the dawn that brings merry delight,
With chuckles and cheer that dance through the light.
We promise to laugh, let our spirits run free,
As dawn's playful spirit awakens with glee!

The Edge of Daylight

At the break of light, I jump in glee,
Chasing shadows, as happy as can be.
My cat's a ninja, leaping high,
While I trip over my own tie.

Sunshine tickles, a playful spark,
It dances wildly, a merry lark.
Coffee spills, my feet are gone,
Guess I should've tied my shoes on!

A pancake flips, then lands like a bird,
My dog is confused, he hasn't heard.
He sniffs at breakfast, a curious face,
While I try to save the syrup's grace.

As dawn rushes in, colors collide,
I wear two socks, what a silly ride!
But laughter blooms, that's my true aim,
In this wild game of morning fame.

Illumination Above the Sea

The sun peeks up, a cheeky grin,
Sailing boats are bobbing, oh what a win!
Seagulls squawk like they own the place,
As I tangle myself in my shoelace.

Waves are giggling, splashing about,
While my sandwich tries to take a route.
A crab wears my flip-flop, snickers loud,
As I chase it in front of a crowd.

Light bounces off the water's gleam,
Will I catch the crab? Hard to beam.
In my sunhat, I look like a fool,
But laughter's the best, that's the rule.

The horizon shimmers, a silly sight,
As I mock-fight with a beach kite.
The day rolls on, absurdly bright,
All in good fun, oh, what a delight!

Glows of Tomorrow

A glow appears, tomorrow's tease,
While I search high, I search low with ease.
I trip on my dreams and tumble down,
But hey, I'm smiling, don't wear a frown!

The stars still twinkle, giggle and sway,
As I dance around in my own clumsy way.
While shadows chuckle, they twist and shout,
I wave my arms in the fun-filled bout.

Tomorrow whispers, "Don't be a bore!"
As I knock over items, oh what a score!
A balloon floats, my head turns slow,
I'm chasing it down, but oh no, oh no!

With every stumble, a laugh doth rise,
Tomorrow's glow, a silly surprise.
So here I am, amidst all this flair,
Just a jester, floating on air.

Dawn's Gentle Caress

Morning arrives with a cheeky wink,
And I fumble for coffee, before I think.
The toaster pops, and I jump back in fright,
As my toast does a jig, what a silly sight!

The cat stretches wide, yawns like the sun,
Wishing to nap, oh, isn't that fun?
While I juggle my cereal, risking a spill,
Dawn's gentle pinch shows my morning skill.

Birds serenade, in the key of loud,
While I shuffle outside, feeling proud.
Slippers on the wrong feet, what a fine flair,
I strut like a peacock, without a care!

So here I am, in the dawn's soft light,
With goofiness glowing, everything is right.
For laughter and joy, that's how you start,
A new day unfolding, a silly art.

Glimmers at Day's End

The sun dips low, it's quite a show,
A bright orange glow, don't miss the flow.
Birds start to sing, as if on cue,
"What shall we do? The sky's asking too!"

A cat on the fence starts a little dance,
Chasing the shadows, oh what a chance!
A squirrel in the tree quips, "Oh, what fun!"
"Let's party all night, till we see the sun!"

The ants march home with snacks galore,
"Don't forget the crumbs!" they excitedly implore.
While twilight giggles, its colors do blend,
Every day ends, but laughs just ascend!

So sit back and chuckle, enjoy the delight,
As day turns to night, oh what a sight!
Let's toast to the twilight, and raise a cheer,
To the silly little things that bring us near!

When Light Touches the Earth

When dawn breaks with glee, the colors collide,
Morning's here early, and it's filled with pride.
The roosters all crow, as if in a race,
To see who can wake up the whole human space!

A rabbit hops by, with a wink and a grin,
"Why are you still sleeping? It's time to begin!"
The sun starts to laugh, spreading rays like confetti,
Even the milkman looks bright and quite petty!

Flowers burst forth in a tangle of cheer,
"What's that? A bee? Oh dear, oh dear!"
They jiggle and wiggle, as bugs buzz around,
"It's a party!" they shout, "Let's dance on the ground!"

So if you should stumble into morning's embrace,
Just join the mish mash of this sun-kissed place.
With laughter and joy as the light takes its turn,
We'll gather the giggles and let our hearts burn!

A Dance of Warmth and Shade

In the park, where laughter hums,
A sunbeam shines, and the ice cream comes.
Kids spin around, each with a balloon,
"Who can catch me? Let's fly to the moon!"

The squirrels applaud with their cheeky moves,
Their little tails dance, oh how it grooves!
A shadow creeps in, with a sly little grin,
"Ready or not, here comes a turtle to win!"

Lazy sunflowers just swaying back and forth,
As if in a contest, boasting their worth.
Little ants parade with snacks on their backs,
"Is this the best day? Now who's up for snacks?"

So let's laugh with glee, and create a parade,
Chasing the sunbeams, we'll never fade!
In the warmth of the light and the shade of the tree,
Join the fun in this dance, wild and free!

The Horizon's Flame

As evening rolls in, a comic delight,
The sky's on fire, what a sight!
Clouds play dress-up in colors so bright,
Even the stars look up with pure fright!

A dog starts to howl, thinks he's in a show,
"Is that my cue? Let's put on a glow!"
The moon chuckles softly, "Give it your best!
Tonight's for the giggles; forget all the rest!"

Fireflies flitter, a twinkling sight,
"Catch me if you can!" They zoom out of sight.
The frogs join in chorus, a croaky refrain,
Singing songs of silliness, happy and plain!

As the curtains of twilight begin to unfurl,
The world turns to laughter, oh what a whirl!
With every last wink from the sun's gentle game,
We celebrate laughter—ah, the horizon's flame!

Rays of New Beginnings

In the morning glow so bright,
My hair stands up, it's quite a sight.
Coffee spills, I chase my cat,
She stares at me like, 'What's up with that?'

Birds are chirping, they think they sing,
I only hope they buy me bling.
A butterfly lands, with flair it struts,
I trip over my own two guts!

The sun is up, it's time to play,
But I lost my pants somewhere today.
Bouncing like a pogo stick,
This morning's laugh is quite the trick!

So here I stand, with breakfast in hand,
On this odd journey, life is quite planned.
With all the giggles and the cheer,
I race to start the day, oh dear!

The Light Beyond the Mist

Fog rolls in, it's thick as stew,
I wave at shadows, is that you?
Tripping on rocks, I've lost my map,
The squirrels are mocking, what a slap!

Luminous orbs in the skies above,
Are those fireflies or stars in love?
I asked a tree about my plight,
It sighed and whispered, 'You'll be alright.'

Through the mist, I spot a glow,
Did I just win the tiny nacho show?
Embellished smiles, I laugh and grin,
The light's just here; let the fun begin!

Yet in this dance with blurred delight,
I might just walk into a cactus bite.
But fun is found behind the haze,
With joy-filled murmurs, I'll sing my praise!

Awakening in Brilliance

Waking up, the sun's a tease,
Stretching limbs like a peaceful breeze.
I lost my socks, they've run away,
I swear they have a party today!

The toast pops up, a mischievous cheer,
Dancing right out of my morning pier.
A spoon decides to join the fun,
Splattering jam, oh, what a run!

Through laughter, the walls start to hum,
I dance with shadows, feeling quite numb.
The blender's spinning with my fate,
It churns my breakfast, oh what a date!

With blissful spirit, I strut my style,
Taking on the world, just for a while.
So bring on the day, the chaos and cheer,
For in this brilliance, I have no fear!

Horizons of Hope and Dreams

Across the fields, the daisies bloom,
They laugh at me as I trip and zoom.
Chasing dreams on a runaway goat,
I thought I'd steer, but he just smote!

Now I'm twirling with flower crowns,
Making friends with the burly hounds.
They roll in mud, and I join too,
We're a mess now, but it's a fun crew!

The sun dips low, like a painted art,
It seems to wink, with a cheeky heart.
With every giggle that lights the air,
I find that laughter is everywhere!

So here's to the day, the faults and glows,
With open arms, I embrace the woes.
In this bright world, I'll chase and scream,
For the joy of life is the wildest dream!

Horizons Awash with Wonder

Birds wear sunglasses, they strut and sway,
Dancing on clouds, in a breezy ballet.
Sunflowers gossip with giggles and cheer,
Whispering secrets only the breeze can hear.

The sun drops in coffee, a splash of delight,
Marshmallows float, soft and white.
A cat steals a slice of that warm apple pie,
And the sky chuckles loud as it waves goodbye.

Balloons bounce along, with faces so bright,
Chasing their shadows in sheer delight.
Lemonade rivers run sweet down the lane,
In this wacky realm where we dance in the rain.

The First Kiss of Day

A rooster in socks gives a crowing cheer,
As jellybeans juggle, tossing without fear.
Tea cups are winking, they giggle and spin,
While pancakes do pirouettes, a fluffy win.

The sun tickles trees with its warm, golden ray,
As squirrels in top hats start their ballet.
With leafy confetti, the branches all sway,
Inviting us into their whimsical play.

With laughter and flapping, it's a sensational sight,
A circus of colors erupts with pure light.
The world wakes up, in such wild disarray,
Welcoming mischief in the dawn's early play.

Pathway of Radiance

A chicken in sneakers struts down the street,
Chasing a taco, oh what a feat!
Rainbows are racing, with giggles galore,
While ice cream cones dream of the flavors in store.

A hopscotch of glitters leads straight to the sky,
Where clouds make pizza that's fluffy and high.
The sun plays charades with the clouds up above,
As the grassholds its breath, waiting for hugs from the dove.

Each step is a shimmy, a jive with surprise,
With ducks in bow ties, and bright bowler hats fly.
This joyous promenade feels like a game,
Where every missed step ignites laughter's flame.

A Morning's Dream Unfolded

The alarm clock hiccups, it's trying to sing,
While socks do the cha-cha, what a morning fling!
Coffee cups start tangoing on the counter,
A merry cacophony, of giggles they flounder.

Toaster pops toast like a triumphant knight,
And muffins do somersaults, oh what a sight!
The blend of laughter fills the air thick,
As waltzing waffles do their party trick.

A sunbeam peeks in with a playful grin,
Inviting the shadows to join in the spin.
With frolic and folly, the day starts anew,
As the rhythm of breakfast delivers its cue.

www.ingramcontent.com/pod-product-compliance
Lightning Source LLC
Chambersburg PA
CBHW072128070526
44585CB00016B/1583